50 Venezuelan Recipes for Home

By: Kelly Johnson

Table of Contents

- Arepas
- Pabellón Criollo
- Hallacas
- Cachapas
- Tequeños
- Patacones
- Asado Negro
- Empanadas
- Polvorosas
- Quesillo
- Mandocas
- Tostones
- Carabina
- Pan de Jamón
- Chupe Andino
- Sopa de Mondongo
- Perico
- Pastel de Chucho
- Dulce de Lechosa
- Torta de Auyama
- Guasacaca
- Ensalada de Pollo
- Cachito
- Pernil
- Bollos Pelones
- Dulce de Leche
- Golfeados
- Tizana
- Cazón en Salsa
- Pabellón Oriental
- Arroz con Leche
- Chivo en Coco
- Tequenos de Hojaldre
- Torta de Piña
- Ceviche de Camarones

- Pata e' Vaca
- Teta e' Monja
- Mandoca de Platano
- Asopado de Mariscos
- Chicha Andina
- Hallaca Andina
- Cocada
- Tigrillo
- Llanero
- Bistec a Caballo
- Guasacaca
- Mandoca de Yuca
- Pastelitos de Chucho
- Hallaca Oriental
- Roscón de Reyes

Arepas

Ingredients:

- 2 cups pre-cooked white cornmeal (Harina P.A.N. is a popular brand)
- 2 1/2 cups warm water
- 1 teaspoon salt
- Vegetable oil, for cooking

Instructions:

1. In a large mixing bowl, combine the pre-cooked white cornmeal and salt.
2. Gradually add the warm water to the cornmeal mixture, stirring continuously until a soft dough forms. The dough should be moist and pliable, but not sticky.
3. Knead the dough for a few minutes until smooth and well combined.
4. Divide the dough into equal-sized portions and shape each portion into a ball.
5. Flatten each dough ball to form a disk about 1/2 inch thick and 3-4 inches in diameter. You can use your hands to shape the arepas or use a tortilla press.
6. Heat a non-stick skillet or griddle over medium heat and lightly grease it with vegetable oil.
7. Place the shaped arepas on the hot skillet and cook for about 5-6 minutes on each side, or until golden brown and cooked through. You may need to adjust the heat to prevent burning.
8. Once cooked, transfer the arepas to a plate lined with paper towels to drain any excess oil.
9. Allow the arepas to cool slightly before slicing them open horizontally with a sharp knife.
10. Serve the arepas warm with your choice of fillings, such as cheese, shredded beef, black beans, avocado, or any other desired toppings.

Enjoy these delicious homemade Venezuelan arepas as a versatile and satisfying meal or snack!

Pabellón Criollo

Ingredients:

- 1 pound flank steak or skirt steak, thinly sliced
- Salt and pepper, to taste
- 2 tablespoons vegetable oil
- 1 onion, chopped
- 2 cloves garlic, minced
- 1 bell pepper, chopped
- 1 can (15 oz) black beans, drained and rinsed
- 1 teaspoon ground cumin
- 1 teaspoon paprika
- 2 cups cooked white rice
- 2 ripe plantains, peeled and sliced diagonally
- Vegetable oil, for frying
- Fresh cilantro, chopped, for garnish (optional)

Instructions:

1. Season the thinly sliced steak with salt and pepper on both sides.
2. In a large skillet, heat the vegetable oil over medium-high heat. Add the seasoned steak slices and cook until browned on both sides, about 3-4 minutes per side. Remove the steak from the skillet and set aside.
3. In the same skillet, add the chopped onion, minced garlic, and chopped bell pepper. Sauté until softened and fragrant, about 5 minutes.
4. Stir in the drained black beans, ground cumin, and paprika. Cook for another 3-4 minutes, mashing some of the beans with the back of a spoon.
5. Return the cooked steak slices to the skillet with the black bean mixture. Stir to combine and let it simmer for a few more minutes until heated through.
6. In a separate skillet, heat vegetable oil over medium heat for frying the plantains. Fry the plantain slices until golden brown and caramelized on both sides, about 2-3 minutes per side. Remove from the skillet and place on a paper towel-lined plate to drain any excess oil.
7. To serve, place a portion of cooked white rice on a plate. Top with the shredded beef and black bean mixture. Arrange the fried plantains alongside.
8. Garnish with fresh chopped cilantro, if desired.
9. Serve the Pabellón Criollo hot and enjoy!

This flavorful and hearty Venezuelan dish is a favorite among locals and visitors alike, showcasing the vibrant and diverse flavors of Venezuelan cuisine.

Hallacas

Ingredients:

For the dough:

- 4 cups pre-cooked white cornmeal (Harina P.A.N. is a popular brand)
- 4 cups warm water
- 1/2 cup vegetable oil or melted lard
- Salt, to taste

For the filling:

- 2 pounds boneless pork shoulder, diced
- 1 pound boneless beef chuck, diced
- 1/2 pound smoked ham, diced
- 1/2 cup raisins
- 1/2 cup pitted green olives, sliced
- 1/2 cup capers
- 2 onions, finely chopped
- 4 cloves garlic, minced
- 1 bell pepper, finely chopped
- 1 cup tomato sauce
- 1/2 cup beef or chicken broth
- 1/2 cup vegetable oil
- 1/4 cup Worcestershire sauce
- 1/4 cup soy sauce
- 1 teaspoon ground cumin
- 1 teaspoon dried oregano
- Salt and pepper, to taste

For assembling and wrapping:

- Plantain leaves, cleaned and softened in hot water
- Butcher's twine or cooking string

Instructions:

For the filling:

1. In a large pot or Dutch oven, heat the vegetable oil over medium heat. Add the onions, garlic, and bell pepper, and sauté until softened and fragrant.
2. Add the diced pork shoulder, beef chuck, and smoked ham to the pot. Cook until browned on all sides.
3. Stir in the tomato sauce, beef or chicken broth, Worcestershire sauce, soy sauce, ground cumin, dried oregano, salt, and pepper. Bring to a simmer.
4. Reduce the heat to low, cover, and let the filling mixture simmer for about 1 1/2 to 2 hours, or until the meat is tender and the flavors have melded together.
5. Stir in the raisins, sliced olives, and capers. Simmer for another 15-20 minutes. Adjust seasoning if necessary. Remove from heat and let it cool.

For the dough:

1. In a large mixing bowl, combine the pre-cooked white cornmeal, warm water, vegetable oil or melted lard, and salt. Mix until a soft and pliable dough forms.
2. Divide the dough into small portions, about the size of a tennis ball.

Assembling and wrapping the Hallacas:

1. Take one portion of dough and spread it onto a softened plantain leaf to form a rectangle.
2. Place a spoonful of the cooled filling mixture onto the center of the dough.
3. Fold the sides of the plantain leaf over the filling, then fold the top and bottom edges to form a rectangular packet.
4. Tie the Hallaca securely with butcher's twine or cooking string.
5. Repeat the process with the remaining dough and filling mixture.
6. Once all Hallacas are assembled, steam them in a large pot or steamer basket for about 1 to 1 1/2 hours, or until the dough is cooked through and firm.

Serving:

1. Allow the Hallacas to cool slightly before unwrapping.
2. Serve the Hallacas warm, either as a main course or as a festive treat during the holiday season.

Enjoy the delicious flavors of this traditional Venezuelan dish!

Cachapas

Ingredients:

- 4 cups fresh corn kernels (about 6-8 ears of corn)
- 1/2 cup cornmeal
- 1/4 cup milk
- 2 tablespoons sugar (adjust to taste)
- Salt, to taste
- Butter or oil, for cooking
- Queso de mano (Venezuelan hand cheese) or mozzarella cheese slices, for serving

Instructions:

1. In a blender or food processor, blend the fresh corn kernels until smooth. You can also use a grater to grate the corn kernels if you prefer a coarser texture.
2. In a large mixing bowl, combine the blended corn, cornmeal, milk, sugar, and salt. Mix well until all ingredients are thoroughly incorporated and you have a smooth batter.
3. Heat a non-stick skillet or griddle over medium heat. Add a small amount of butter or oil to grease the surface.
4. Pour about 1/4 cup of the batter onto the hot skillet, spreading it out slightly to form a round shape.
5. Cook the cachapa for 2-3 minutes on each side, or until golden brown and cooked through. You'll know it's ready to flip when bubbles start to form on the surface and the edges begin to set.
6. Repeat the process with the remaining batter, adding more butter or oil to the skillet as needed.
7. Serve the cachapas warm, topped with slices of Queso de mano or mozzarella cheese. You can also serve them with butter, cream, or any other savory fillings of your choice.

Enjoy these delicious and comforting cachapas as a snack, breakfast, or part of a savory meal!

Tequeños

Ingredients:

- 1 package of pre-made empanada dough (or you can make your own dough)
- 1 pound (450g) queso blanco or mozzarella cheese, cut into sticks
- Vegetable oil, for frying

Instructions:

1. If using pre-made empanada dough, allow it to thaw according to package instructions. If making your own dough, prepare the dough and let it rest for about 30 minutes.
2. Cut the queso blanco or mozzarella cheese into sticks, about 3 inches long and 1/2 inch thick.
3. Take a piece of dough and roll it out into a thin circle or rectangle, depending on the shape of your dough.
4. Place a cheese stick on one end of the dough and roll it up tightly, making sure to seal the edges so that the cheese doesn't ooze out during frying. Repeat with the remaining dough and cheese sticks.
5. Heat vegetable oil in a deep skillet or pot to 350°F (180°C).
6. Carefully place the tequeños in the hot oil, a few at a time, making sure not to overcrowd the skillet.
7. Fry the tequeños until they are golden brown and crispy on all sides, about 2-3 minutes per side.
8. Once cooked, remove the tequeños from the oil and place them on a plate lined with paper towels to drain any excess oil.
9. Serve the tequeños hot with your favorite dipping sauce, such as guasacaca (avocado sauce) or salsa rosada (pink sauce).

Enjoy these delicious and addictive tequeños as a snack or appetizer at your next gathering or as a treat for yourself!

Patacones

Ingredients:

- 2 green plantains
- Vegetable oil, for frying
- Salt, to taste
- Optional: garlic salt, seasoning salt, or other seasonings of your choice

Instructions:

1. Peel the green plantains and cut them into 1-inch thick slices.
2. Heat vegetable oil in a deep skillet or pot over medium-high heat until it reaches about 350°F (180°C).
3. Carefully add the plantain slices to the hot oil and fry them for about 2-3 minutes on each side, or until they are lightly golden brown.
4. Remove the fried plantain slices from the oil and place them on a paper towel-lined plate to drain any excess oil.
5. Using a tostonera (plantain press) or the bottom of a flat, heavy object such as a plate or glass, flatten each fried plantain slice to about 1/4 inch thickness.
6. Return the flattened plantain slices to the hot oil and fry them again for another 2-3 minutes on each side, or until they are crispy and golden brown.
7. Remove the patacones from the oil and place them back on the paper towel-lined plate to drain any excess oil.
8. Sprinkle the patacones with salt (and any other seasonings of your choice) while they are still hot.
9. Serve the patacones hot as a side dish or snack, accompanied by your favorite dipping sauce or salsa.

Enjoy these crispy and delicious patacones as a tasty and addictive snack or side dish!

Asado Negro

Ingredients:

- 2 pounds beef eye of round or flank steak, cut into chunks
- Salt and pepper, to taste
- 1/4 cup vegetable oil
- 1 onion, chopped
- 1 bell pepper, chopped
- 4 cloves garlic, minced
- 1 cup beef broth
- 1 cup red wine
- 1/4 cup Worcestershire sauce
- 2 tablespoons brown sugar
- 2 tablespoons balsamic vinegar
- 1 teaspoon ground cumin
- 1 teaspoon dried thyme
- 1/2 teaspoon ground cinnamon
- 1/2 teaspoon ground cloves
- 1/4 teaspoon ground nutmeg
- 1 bay leaf
- 1 tablespoon cornstarch (optional, for thickening)
- 2 tablespoons water (optional, for cornstarch slurry)
- Cooked white rice, for serving
- Sliced ripe plantains, for serving

Instructions:

1. Season the beef chunks with salt and pepper to taste.
2. In a large Dutch oven or heavy-bottomed pot, heat the vegetable oil over medium-high heat. Add the seasoned beef chunks and brown them on all sides, working in batches if necessary. Remove the browned beef from the pot and set aside.
3. In the same pot, add the chopped onion, bell pepper, and minced garlic. Sauté until the vegetables are softened and fragrant.
4. Return the browned beef chunks to the pot, along with any accumulated juices.
5. Pour in the beef broth, red wine, Worcestershire sauce, brown sugar, balsamic vinegar, ground cumin, dried thyme, ground cinnamon, ground cloves, ground nutmeg, and bay leaf. Stir to combine.

6. Bring the mixture to a simmer, then reduce the heat to low. Cover and let the beef simmer gently for about 2-3 hours, or until the meat is tender and the sauce has thickened.
7. If desired, you can thicken the sauce further by making a cornstarch slurry. In a small bowl, mix together the cornstarch and water until smooth. Stir the slurry into the simmering sauce and cook for an additional 5-10 minutes, or until thickened to your liking.
8. Once the beef is tender and the sauce has thickened to your desired consistency, remove the bay leaf from the pot.
9. Serve the Asado Negro hot over cooked white rice, accompanied by sliced ripe plantains.

Enjoy the rich and aromatic flavors of this classic Venezuelan dish, Asado Negro, served as a comforting and satisfying meal!

Empanadas

Ingredients:

For the dough:

- 3 cups all-purpose flour
- 1 teaspoon salt
- 1/2 cup unsalted butter, cold and cut into small pieces
- 1 egg
- 1/2 cup cold water

For the filling:

- 1 tablespoon vegetable oil
- 1 onion, finely chopped
- 2 cloves garlic, minced
- 1 pound ground beef
- 1 teaspoon ground cumin
- 1 teaspoon paprika
- 1/2 teaspoon chili powder (optional, for extra heat)
- Salt and pepper, to taste
- 1/4 cup chopped green olives
- 1/4 cup raisins
- 2 hard-boiled eggs, chopped

Instructions:

For the dough:

1. In a large mixing bowl, combine the flour and salt. Add the cold butter pieces and use your fingers or a pastry cutter to cut the butter into the flour until the mixture resembles coarse crumbs.
2. In a small bowl, whisk together the egg and cold water. Gradually add the egg mixture to the flour mixture, stirring until a dough forms. You may not need to use all of the egg mixture.

3. Turn the dough out onto a lightly floured surface and knead it gently until smooth. Shape the dough into a ball, wrap it in plastic wrap, and refrigerate for at least 30 minutes.

For the filling:

1. Heat the vegetable oil in a large skillet over medium heat. Add the chopped onion and minced garlic, and sauté until softened and fragrant.
2. Add the ground beef to the skillet and cook until browned, breaking it up with a spoon as it cooks.
3. Stir in the ground cumin, paprika, chili powder (if using), salt, and pepper. Cook for another minute to toast the spices.
4. Remove the skillet from the heat and stir in the chopped green olives, raisins, and chopped hard-boiled eggs. Set the filling aside to cool.

Assembling the empanadas:

1. Preheat your oven to 375°F (190°C). Line a baking sheet with parchment paper.
2. On a lightly floured surface, roll out the chilled dough to about 1/8 inch thickness. Use a round cutter or a small plate to cut out circles of dough.
3. Place a spoonful of the cooled beef filling in the center of each dough circle.
4. Fold the dough over the filling to create a half-moon shape. Use a fork to crimp the edges of the empanadas to seal them shut.
5. Place the assembled empanadas on the prepared baking sheet. Brush the tops of the empanadas with beaten egg or milk for a golden finish, if desired.
6. Bake the empanadas in the preheated oven for 20-25 minutes, or until golden brown and crispy.

Enjoy these homemade beef empanadas warm as a delicious snack, appetizer, or meal!

You can also customize the filling with your favorite ingredients, such as cheese, vegetables, or different types of meat.

Polvorosas

Ingredients:

- 1 cup unsalted butter, softened
- 1 cup powdered sugar, plus extra for coating
- 1 teaspoon vanilla extract
- 2 cups all-purpose flour
- 1/4 teaspoon salt
- Optional: additional powdered sugar for dusting

Instructions:

1. Preheat your oven to 350°F (175°C). Line a baking sheet with parchment paper.
2. In a large mixing bowl, cream together the softened butter and powdered sugar until light and fluffy.
3. Add the vanilla extract and mix until well combined.
4. Gradually add the flour and salt to the butter mixture, mixing until a soft dough forms. The dough should be slightly crumbly but hold together when pressed.
5. Shape the dough into small balls, about 1 inch in diameter. Roll each ball in powdered sugar until well coated.
6. Place the coated dough balls on the prepared baking sheet, leaving some space between each cookie.
7. Use a fork to gently press down on the top of each cookie to flatten it slightly and create a crisscross pattern.
8. Bake the Polvorosas in the preheated oven for 12-15 minutes, or until the edges are lightly golden.
9. Remove the cookies from the oven and let them cool on the baking sheet for a few minutes before transferring them to a wire rack to cool completely.
10. Once cooled, you can dust the Polvorosas with additional powdered sugar if desired.

Enjoy these delicate and crumbly Polvorosas with a cup of coffee or tea as a delightful treat! They're perfect for sharing with friends and family or for enjoying as a sweet snack anytime.

Quesillo

Ingredients:

For the caramel:

- 1 cup granulated sugar
- 1/4 cup water

For the custard:

- 4 large eggs
- 1 can (14 oz) sweetened condensed milk
- 1 can (12 oz) evaporated milk
- 1 teaspoon vanilla extract

Instructions:

1. Preheat your oven to 350°F (175°C). Place a baking dish or roasting pan filled with about 1 inch of water in the oven to create a water bath for baking the quesillo.
2. In a small saucepan, combine the granulated sugar and water for the caramel. Heat over medium heat, stirring occasionally, until the sugar has dissolved.
3. Increase the heat to medium-high and let the mixture come to a boil without stirring. Cook until the caramel turns a deep golden brown color, swirling the pan occasionally to ensure even cooking.
4. Once the caramel reaches the desired color, immediately pour it into the bottom of a 9-inch round cake pan or mold, tilting the pan to coat the bottom evenly. Be careful as the caramel will be very hot. Set aside to cool and harden.
5. In a blender or food processor, combine the eggs, sweetened condensed milk, evaporated milk, and vanilla extract. Blend until smooth and well combined.
6. Pour the custard mixture over the hardened caramel in the cake pan or mold.
7. Carefully transfer the cake pan or mold to the preheated oven and place it in the water bath.
8. Bake the quesillo for 50-60 minutes, or until set around the edges but still slightly jiggly in the center.

9. Remove the quesillo from the oven and let it cool to room temperature. Then, cover and refrigerate for at least 4 hours or overnight to chill and firm up.
10. To serve, run a knife around the edge of the quesillo to loosen it from the pan. Place a serving plate over the top of the pan and quickly invert it to release the quesillo onto the plate. The caramel will flow over the top, creating a beautiful glaze.
11. Slice the quesillo and serve chilled.

Enjoy this creamy and decadent Quesillo as a delicious dessert to share with friends and family!

Mandocas

Ingredients:

- 2 ripe plantains, peeled and grated
- 2 cups pre-cooked white cornmeal (Harina P.A.N. is a popular brand)
- 1/4 cup granulated sugar (adjust to taste)
- 1/2 teaspoon salt
- 1 teaspoon ground cinnamon (optional)
- 1/2 cup milk
- Vegetable oil, for frying

Instructions:

1. In a large mixing bowl, combine the grated ripe plantains, pre-cooked white cornmeal, granulated sugar, salt, and ground cinnamon (if using).
2. Gradually add the milk to the mixture, stirring until a soft and pliable dough forms. The dough should be moist but not too sticky. If necessary, adjust the consistency by adding more milk or cornmeal.
3. Divide the dough into equal-sized portions and shape each portion into a ball.
4. Flatten each dough ball slightly to form a disc, about 1/2 inch thick.
5. Heat vegetable oil in a deep skillet or pot over medium heat until it reaches about 350°F (175°C).
6. Carefully add the flattened dough discs to the hot oil, a few at a time, without overcrowding the skillet.
7. Fry the mandocas until they are golden brown and crispy on both sides, about 3-4 minutes per side.
8. Once cooked, remove the mandocas from the oil and place them on a paper towel-lined plate to drain any excess oil.
9. Serve the mandocas warm, either plain or accompanied by cheese, butter, or other toppings of your choice.

Enjoy these delicious and comforting mandocas as a delightful breakfast treat or snack, perfect for any time of the day!

Tostones

Ingredients:

- 2 green plantains
- Vegetable oil, for frying
- Salt, to taste
- Optional: garlic salt, seasoning salt, or other seasonings of your choice

Instructions:

1. Peel the green plantains and cut them into 1-inch thick slices.
2. Heat vegetable oil in a deep skillet or pot over medium-high heat until it reaches about 350°F (175°C).
3. Carefully add the plantain slices to the hot oil and fry them for about 2-3 minutes on each side, or until they're lightly golden brown.
4. Remove the fried plantain slices from the oil and place them on a paper towel-lined plate to drain any excess oil.
5. Using a tostonera (plantain press) or the bottom of a flat, heavy object such as a plate or glass, flatten each fried plantain slice to about 1/4 inch thickness.
6. Return the flattened plantain slices to the hot oil and fry them again for another 2-3 minutes on each side, or until they're crispy and golden brown.
7. Remove the tostones from the oil and place them back on the paper towel-lined plate to drain any excess oil.
8. Sprinkle the tostones with salt (and any other seasonings of your choice) while they're still hot.
9. Serve the tostones hot as a side dish or snack, accompanied by your favorite dipping sauce or salsa.

Enjoy these crispy and delicious tostones as a tasty and addictive snack or side dish!

They pair well with a variety of toppings and are perfect for sharing with friends and family.

Carabina

Ingredients:

- 1 pound ground beef
- 1 onion, finely chopped
- 2 cloves garlic, minced
- 1 bell pepper, diced
- 1 tablespoon vegetable oil
- 1 teaspoon ground cumin
- 1 teaspoon paprika
- Salt and pepper, to taste
- 1 cup cooked black beans
- 1 cup corn kernels (fresh or frozen)
- 1 cup cooked rice
- 1 cup shredded cheese (such as queso blanco or mozzarella)
- 1/4 cup chopped fresh cilantro (optional, for garnish)
- Sliced avocado, for serving (optional)

Instructions:

1. In a large skillet, heat the vegetable oil over medium heat. Add the chopped onion, minced garlic, and diced bell pepper. Sauté until the vegetables are softened and fragrant, about 5 minutes.
2. Add the ground beef to the skillet and cook until browned, breaking it up with a spoon as it cooks.
3. Stir in the ground cumin, paprika, salt, and pepper. Cook for another minute to toast the spices.
4. Add the cooked black beans and corn kernels to the skillet, stirring to combine. Cook for an additional 5 minutes, until heated through.
5. To serve, spoon the cooked rice onto plates or bowls. Top with the beef and bean mixture, then sprinkle with shredded cheese.
6. Garnish with chopped fresh cilantro, if desired, and serve with sliced avocado on the side.

This fictional "Carabina" recipe combines savory ground beef with beans, corn, and rice, creating a hearty and flavorful dish that's perfect for a satisfying meal. Feel free to adjust the ingredients and seasonings according to your taste preferences. Enjoy your culinary creation!

Pan de Jamón

Ingredients:

For the dough:

- 4 cups all-purpose flour
- 1/4 cup granulated sugar
- 1 teaspoon salt
- 2 1/4 teaspoons active dry yeast
- 1/2 cup warm water (110°F/45°C)
- 1/2 cup whole milk, warmed
- 1/4 cup unsalted butter, melted
- 2 large eggs

For the filling:

- 1/2 pound thinly sliced ham
- 1/2 pound thinly sliced cooked bacon
- 1 cup pitted green olives, halved
- 1/2 cup raisins

Instructions:

For the dough:

1. In a small bowl, dissolve the active dry yeast in warm water and let it sit for about 5 minutes until frothy.
2. In a large mixing bowl, combine the flour, sugar, and salt.
3. Add the warm milk, melted butter, eggs, and yeast mixture to the dry ingredients. Mix until a dough forms.
4. Knead the dough on a floured surface for about 5-7 minutes until smooth and elastic.
5. Place the dough in a greased bowl, cover with a clean kitchen towel, and let it rise in a warm place for about 1-2 hours, or until doubled in size.

Assembling the Pan de Jamón:

1. Punch down the risen dough and divide it into two equal portions.
2. Roll out each portion into a rectangle, about 1/4 inch thick.
3. Arrange half of the thinly sliced ham and bacon over each rectangle of dough, leaving a small border around the edges.
4. Sprinkle half of the halved olives and raisins evenly over the ham and bacon.
5. Starting from one long edge, roll up each rectangle of dough tightly to form a log.
6. Place the rolled dough logs seam side down on a baking sheet lined with parchment paper.
7. Cover the shaped Pan de Jamón with a clean kitchen towel and let them rise for another 30-45 minutes.

Baking the Pan de Jamón:

1. Preheat your oven to 350°F (175°C).
2. Bake the Pan de Jamón in the preheated oven for 30-35 minutes, or until golden brown and cooked through.
3. Remove the baked Pan de Jamón from the oven and let them cool slightly before slicing and serving.

Enjoy this delicious and festive Pan de Jamón with your loved ones during the holiday season or any special occasion!

Chupe Andino

Ingredients:

- 2 tablespoons vegetable oil
- 1 onion, finely chopped
- 2 cloves garlic, minced
- 2 medium carrots, diced
- 2 medium potatoes, peeled and diced
- 2 ears of corn, kernels removed (or 1 cup frozen corn kernels)
- 1/2 cup green peas (fresh or frozen)
- 4 cups chicken or vegetable broth
- 1 cup evaporated milk
- 1 cup shredded cheese (such as queso fresco, mozzarella, or cheddar)
- 4 large eggs
- 1/4 cup chopped fresh cilantro or parsley
- Salt and pepper, to taste

Instructions:

1. In a large pot or Dutch oven, heat the vegetable oil over medium heat. Add the chopped onion and minced garlic, and sauté until softened and fragrant.
2. Add the diced carrots and potatoes to the pot, and cook for a few minutes until they begin to soften.
3. Stir in the corn kernels and green peas, and cook for another few minutes.
4. Pour in the chicken or vegetable broth, and bring the mixture to a simmer. Let it cook for about 15-20 minutes, or until the vegetables are tender.
5. Stir in the evaporated milk and shredded cheese until the cheese is melted and the soup is creamy.
6. Crack the eggs into the soup, spacing them out evenly. Cover the pot and let the eggs poach in the soup for about 5-7 minutes, or until the egg whites are set but the yolks are still runny.
7. Season the soup with salt and pepper to taste, and sprinkle chopped cilantro or parsley over the top.
8. Ladle the Chupe Andino into bowls, making sure to include an egg in each serving.
9. Serve hot and enjoy!

This Chupe Andino recipe offers a delicious taste of the Andean region's culinary tradition, combining creamy soup with hearty vegetables and eggs for a satisfying meal. Adjust the ingredients and seasonings according to your taste preferences, and feel free to add other Andean ingredients such as quinoa or aji amarillo for extra flavor.

Sopa de Mondongo

Ingredients:

- 1 pound beef tripe, cleaned and cut into small pieces
- 1 tablespoon vegetable oil
- 1 onion, finely chopped
- 2 cloves garlic, minced
- 2 medium carrots, diced
- 2 medium potatoes, peeled and diced
- 1 bell pepper, diced
- 1 tomato, diced
- 1/4 cup chopped cilantro
- 8 cups beef or chicken broth
- Salt and pepper, to taste
- Optional: 1/2 teaspoon ground cumin, 1/2 teaspoon dried oregano, 1/4 teaspoon paprika
- Lime wedges, for serving
- Cooked white rice, for serving

Instructions:

1. In a large pot, bring water to a boil. Add the beef tripe pieces and boil for about 10 minutes. Drain the tripe and rinse it under cold water. Set aside.
2. In the same pot, heat the vegetable oil over medium heat. Add the chopped onion and minced garlic, and sauté until softened and fragrant.
3. Add the diced carrots, potatoes, bell pepper, and tomato to the pot, and cook for a few minutes until they begin to soften.
4. Stir in the beef or chicken broth and bring the mixture to a simmer.
5. Add the boiled tripe pieces to the pot, along with chopped cilantro and any optional seasonings such as ground cumin, dried oregano, and paprika.
6. Reduce the heat to low, cover the pot, and let the soup simmer for about 1 to 1.5 hours, or until the tripe is tender and the flavors have melded together.
7. Season the soup with salt and pepper to taste.
8. Serve the Sopa de Mondongo hot, garnished with additional chopped cilantro if desired, and accompanied by lime wedges and cooked white rice on the side.

Enjoy this hearty and comforting Sopa de Mondongo as a delicious and satisfying meal! Adjust the seasonings and ingredients according to your taste preferences.

Perico

Ingredients:

- 4 large eggs
- 1 tablespoon vegetable oil or butter
- 1 small onion, finely chopped
- 1 tomato, seeded and finely chopped
- Salt and pepper, to taste
- Chopped fresh cilantro or parsley, for garnish (optional)

Instructions:

1. Crack the eggs into a bowl and whisk them until well beaten. Season with salt and pepper to taste.
2. Heat the vegetable oil or butter in a non-stick skillet over medium heat.
3. Add the chopped onion to the skillet and sauté until softened and translucent, about 3-4 minutes.
4. Add the chopped tomato to the skillet and cook for another 2-3 minutes, until the tomato has softened slightly.
5. Pour the beaten eggs into the skillet with the onions and tomatoes. Let the eggs cook for a few seconds undisturbed until they start to set around the edges.
6. Using a spatula, gently push the cooked edges of the eggs towards the center of the skillet, allowing the uncooked eggs to flow to the edges. Continue cooking and gently stirring the eggs until they are softly scrambled and cooked to your desired consistency.
7. Remove the skillet from the heat and transfer the scrambled eggs to a serving plate.
8. Garnish the Perico with chopped fresh cilantro or parsley, if desired.
9. Serve the Perico hot with arepas, bread, or your favorite breakfast accompaniments.

Enjoy this delicious and simple Venezuelan breakfast dish, Perico, as a satisfying start to your day!

Pastel de Chucho

Ingredients:

- 2 pounds chucho fish fillets, cooked and shredded (you can use any firm white fish as a substitute)
- 2 ripe plantains, peeled and sliced lengthwise
- 1 onion, finely chopped
- 2 cloves garlic, minced
- 1 bell pepper, diced
- 1 tomato, diced
- 1 cup fish or vegetable broth
- 1/2 cup coconut milk
- 2 tablespoons vegetable oil
- 1/4 cup all-purpose flour
- 1/4 cup chopped fresh cilantro
- Salt and pepper, to taste
- Sliced avocado, for serving (optional)

Instructions:

1. Preheat your oven to 350°F (175°C). Grease a baking dish with oil or cooking spray.
2. In a large skillet, heat the vegetable oil over medium heat. Add the chopped onion, minced garlic, and diced bell pepper, and sauté until softened and fragrant.
3. Add the diced tomato to the skillet and cook for another 2-3 minutes, until the tomato has softened.
4. Sprinkle the flour over the vegetables in the skillet and cook, stirring constantly, for about 1 minute to make a roux.
5. Gradually pour in the fish or vegetable broth and coconut milk, stirring constantly to prevent lumps from forming. Cook for a few minutes until the sauce thickens slightly.
6. Add the shredded chucho fish to the skillet, stirring to coat it evenly with the sauce. Cook for another 2-3 minutes, then remove the skillet from the heat.
7. Arrange a layer of sliced plantains on the bottom of the greased baking dish. Spoon half of the fish mixture over the plantains.
8. Repeat the layers with the remaining plantains and fish mixture.

9. Cover the baking dish with aluminum foil and bake in the preheated oven for 30-35 minutes, or until the casserole is heated through and the plantains are tender.
10. Remove the foil from the baking dish and sprinkle chopped fresh cilantro over the top of the casserole.
11. Serve the Pastel de Chucho hot, garnished with sliced avocado if desired.

Enjoy this flavorful and comforting Venezuelan coastal dish, Pastel de Chucho, as a delicious main course!

Dulce de Lechosa

Ingredients:

- 1 green papaya (about 2-3 pounds), peeled, seeded, and thinly sliced
- 4 cups water
- 3 cups granulated sugar
- 1 cinnamon stick
- 3 whole cloves
- 1 tablespoon lime juice
- 1 teaspoon vanilla extract
- Optional: grated lime zest, for garnish

Instructions:

1. Place the thinly sliced green papaya in a large bowl and cover it with cold water. Let it soak for about 1-2 hours to reduce bitterness. Drain and rinse the papaya slices thoroughly.
2. In a large pot, combine the soaked papaya slices, water, granulated sugar, cinnamon stick, and whole cloves.
3. Bring the mixture to a boil over medium-high heat, then reduce the heat to low and let it simmer gently for about 45-60 minutes, stirring occasionally, until the papaya slices are translucent and tender.
4. Remove the pot from the heat and stir in the lime juice and vanilla extract.
5. Let the Dulce de Lechosa cool to room temperature in the pot. The syrup will thicken as it cools.
6. Once cooled, transfer the Dulce de Lechosa to serving bowls or jars. You can serve it warm or chilled.
7. Garnish with grated lime zest, if desired, before serving.

Enjoy this sweet and aromatic Dulce de Lechosa as a delightful dessert or snack, perfect for sharing with friends and family! It's a lovely way to enjoy the unique flavor of green papaya.

Torta de Auyama

Ingredients:

- 2 cups all-purpose flour
- 2 teaspoons baking powder
- 1 teaspoon baking soda
- 1/2 teaspoon salt
- 1 teaspoon ground cinnamon
- 1/2 teaspoon ground nutmeg
- 1/4 teaspoon ground cloves
- 1 cup granulated sugar
- 1/2 cup brown sugar
- 1/2 cup vegetable oil
- 3 large eggs
- 1 teaspoon vanilla extract
- 2 cups mashed pumpkin (auyama), cooked and cooled
- 1/2 cup chopped walnuts or pecans (optional)
- Powdered sugar, for dusting (optional)

Instructions:

1. Preheat your oven to 350°F (175°C). Grease and flour a 9-inch round cake pan or line it with parchment paper.
2. In a medium bowl, sift together the all-purpose flour, baking powder, baking soda, salt, ground cinnamon, ground nutmeg, and ground cloves. Set aside.
3. In a large mixing bowl, combine the granulated sugar, brown sugar, and vegetable oil. Mix until well combined.
4. Add the eggs, one at a time, beating well after each addition. Stir in the vanilla extract.
5. Gradually add the mashed pumpkin (auyama) to the wet ingredients, mixing until smooth and well incorporated.
6. Gradually add the dry ingredients to the wet ingredients, mixing until just combined. Be careful not to overmix.
7. If using, fold in the chopped walnuts or pecans until evenly distributed throughout the batter.
8. Pour the batter into the prepared cake pan and smooth the top with a spatula.
9. Bake in the preheated oven for 35-40 minutes, or until a toothpick inserted into the center of the cake comes out clean.

10. Remove the cake from the oven and let it cool in the pan for 10 minutes before transferring it to a wire rack to cool completely.
11. Once cooled, dust the top of the cake with powdered sugar, if desired.
12. Slice and serve the Torta de Auyama as a delicious dessert or snack.

Enjoy this moist and flavorful Torta de Auyama with a cup of coffee or tea for a delightful treat! It's perfect for celebrating the flavors of pumpkin in a delicious cake.

Guasacaca

Ingredients:

- 2 ripe avocados, peeled and pitted
- 1 small onion, finely chopped
- 2 cloves garlic, minced
- 1/4 cup fresh cilantro, chopped
- 2 tablespoons white vinegar or lime juice
- 1 tablespoon olive oil
- Salt and pepper, to taste
- Optional: 1/2 to 1 jalapeño or serrano pepper, seeded and finely chopped (for extra heat)

Instructions:

1. In a medium bowl, mash the ripe avocados with a fork until smooth, leaving some small chunks if desired for texture.
2. Add the finely chopped onion, minced garlic, chopped cilantro, white vinegar or lime juice, and olive oil to the mashed avocados.
3. If using, add the chopped jalapeño or serrano pepper for a bit of heat.
4. Season the Guasacaca with salt and pepper to taste, and stir until all the ingredients are well combined.
5. Taste and adjust the seasoning, adding more salt, pepper, or vinegar/lime juice if needed.
6. Cover the Guasacaca with plastic wrap, pressing it directly onto the surface to prevent browning, and refrigerate for at least 30 minutes to allow the flavors to meld.
7. Serve the Guasacaca as a dip for tortilla chips, or as a condiment with grilled meats, arepas, empanadas, or other dishes.

Enjoy this delicious and versatile Guasacaca sauce as a flavorful addition to your favorite Venezuelan or Latin American dishes! Adjust the ingredients and seasonings according to your taste preferences.

Ensalada de Pollo

Ingredients:

- 2 cups cooked chicken breast, shredded or diced
- 1/2 cup celery, finely chopped
- 1/2 cup red onion, finely chopped
- 1/2 cup bell pepper (any color), diced
- 1/4 cup fresh parsley, chopped
- 1/4 cup mayonnaise
- 2 tablespoons plain Greek yogurt (or sour cream)
- 1 tablespoon Dijon mustard
- 1 tablespoon lemon juice (or lime juice)
- Salt and pepper, to taste
- Optional: chopped nuts (such as almonds or pecans), dried cranberries, grapes, or apples for added texture and flavor

Instructions:

1. In a large mixing bowl, combine the cooked chicken breast, chopped celery, red onion, bell pepper, and fresh parsley.
2. In a separate small bowl, whisk together the mayonnaise, Greek yogurt (or sour cream), Dijon mustard, and lemon juice until smooth and well combined.
3. Pour the dressing over the chicken and vegetable mixture, and toss gently until everything is evenly coated.
4. Season the Ensalada de Pollo with salt and pepper to taste, and adjust the seasoning if needed.
5. If using, add any optional ingredients such as chopped nuts, dried cranberries, grapes, or apples for extra texture and flavor. Mix gently to incorporate.
6. Cover the Ensalada de Pollo and refrigerate for at least 30 minutes to allow the flavors to meld and the salad to chill.
7. Serve the Ensalada de Pollo chilled as a side dish, appetizer, or main course.

Enjoy this delicious and refreshing Ensalada de Pollo on its own, as a sandwich filling, or served over a bed of greens for a light and satisfying meal! Feel free to customize the salad with your favorite ingredients and adjust the dressing according to your taste preferences.

Cachito

Ingredients:

- 4 cups all-purpose flour
- 1/4 cup granulated sugar
- 1 teaspoon salt
- 2 1/4 teaspoons active dry yeast
- 1/2 cup warm water (110°F/45°C)
- 1/2 cup whole milk, warmed
- 1/4 cup unsalted butter, melted
- 2 large eggs
- 8 slices ham, thinly sliced
- 1 cup shredded cheese (such as mozzarella or cheddar)
- Optional: 1 egg, beaten (for egg wash)

Instructions:

1. In a small bowl, dissolve the active dry yeast in warm water and let it sit for about 5 minutes until frothy.
2. In a large mixing bowl, combine the flour, sugar, and salt.
3. Add the warm milk, melted butter, eggs, and yeast mixture to the dry ingredients. Mix until a dough forms.
4. Knead the dough on a floured surface for about 5-7 minutes until smooth and elastic.
5. Place the dough in a greased bowl, cover with a clean kitchen towel, and let it rise in a warm place for about 1-2 hours, or until doubled in size.
6. Preheat your oven to 375°F (190°C). Line a baking sheet with parchment paper.
7. Punch down the risen dough and divide it into 8 equal portions.
8. Roll out each portion of dough into an oval shape, about 1/4 inch thick.
9. Place a slice of ham and a sprinkle of shredded cheese on each oval of dough.
10. Starting from one long edge, roll up each oval of dough tightly to form a log, enclosing the ham and cheese filling.
11. Place the rolled cachitos on the prepared baking sheet, seam side down, leaving space between each one.
12. Optional: Brush the tops of the cachitos with beaten egg for a golden finish.
13. Bake in the preheated oven for 15-20 minutes, or until the cachitos are golden brown and cooked through.
14. Remove the cachitos from the oven and let them cool slightly before serving.

Enjoy these delicious and savory Cachitos as a delightful breakfast or snack, perfect for any time of the day!

Pernil

Ingredients:

- 1 bone-in pork shoulder (also known as pork butt or picnic shoulder), about 5-7 pounds
- 6 cloves garlic, minced
- 1/4 cup orange juice
- 1/4 cup lime juice
- 1/4 cup olive oil
- 2 tablespoons white vinegar
- 2 tablespoons dried oregano
- 2 tablespoons ground cumin
- 1 tablespoon paprika
- 1 tablespoon salt
- 1 teaspoon black pepper

Instructions:

1. In a small bowl, combine the minced garlic, orange juice, lime juice, olive oil, white vinegar, dried oregano, ground cumin, paprika, salt, and black pepper to make the marinade.
2. Place the pork shoulder in a large roasting pan or baking dish. Using a sharp knife, score the surface of the pork in a crosshatch pattern, making shallow cuts about 1 inch apart.
3. Pour the marinade over the pork shoulder, making sure to rub it into all the nooks and crannies and coat the meat thoroughly.
4. Cover the roasting pan with plastic wrap and marinate the pork in the refrigerator for at least 4 hours, or preferably overnight, to allow the flavors to penetrate the meat.
5. Preheat your oven to 325°F (160°C). Remove the plastic wrap from the roasting pan and cover the pan tightly with aluminum foil.
6. Roast the pork shoulder in the preheated oven for about 4-5 hours, or until the meat is tender and easily pulls apart with a fork.
7. Remove the foil from the roasting pan and increase the oven temperature to 425°F (220°C). Return the pork shoulder to the oven and continue roasting, uncovered, for an additional 30 minutes, or until the skin is crispy and golden brown.

8. Once the pernil is done, remove it from the oven and let it rest for about 15-20 minutes before slicing and serving.

Enjoy this flavorful and aromatic Pernil as a main dish for your next festive gathering or special occasion! Serve it with rice, beans, roasted vegetables, or your favorite side dishes for a delicious and satisfying meal.

Bollos Pelones

Ingredients:

For the dough:

- 2 cups pre-cooked white cornmeal (masarepa)
- 2 cups warm water
- 1 teaspoon salt
- 1 tablespoon vegetable oil

For the filling:

- 1 pound ground beef or shredded cooked beef
- 1 onion, finely chopped
- 2 cloves garlic, minced
- 1 bell pepper, finely chopped
- 1 tomato, finely chopped
- 1 tablespoon vegetable oil
- 1 teaspoon ground cumin
- 1 teaspoon paprika
- Salt and pepper, to taste

Instructions:

For the filling:

1. In a large skillet, heat the vegetable oil over medium heat. Add the chopped onion, minced garlic, and bell pepper, and sauté until softened and fragrant.
2. Add the ground beef (or shredded cooked beef) to the skillet and cook until browned, breaking it up with a spoon as it cooks.
3. Stir in the chopped tomato, ground cumin, paprika, salt, and pepper. Cook for another 5-7 minutes, until the mixture is well combined and the flavors have melded together. Remove from heat and set aside.

For the dough:

1. In a large mixing bowl, combine the pre-cooked white cornmeal (masarepa) and salt.
2. Gradually add the warm water, mixing with your hands until a soft dough forms.
3. Divide the dough into equal portions and shape each portion into a ball.

Assembling the Bollos Pelones:

1. Take one portion of the dough and flatten it into a round disc in the palm of your hand.
2. Place a spoonful of the meat filling in the center of the dough disc.
3. Carefully wrap the dough around the filling, shaping it into a smooth ball with the meat completely enclosed.
4. Repeat with the remaining dough and filling.

Cooking the Bollos Pelones:

1. Fill a large pot with water and bring it to a boil over high heat.
2. Carefully drop the bollos pelones into the boiling water, making sure they are fully submerged.
3. Reduce the heat to medium-low and let the bollos pelones simmer for about 30-40 minutes, or until cooked through and firm.
4. Use a slotted spoon to remove the bollos pelones from the water and drain them on a plate lined with paper towels.
5. Serve the bollos pelones hot as a delicious and satisfying meal or snack.

Enjoy these flavorful Bollos Pelones as a comforting and hearty dish, perfect for any occasion!

Dulce de Leche

Ingredients:

- 1 can (14 ounces) sweetened condensed milk

Instructions:

1. Pour the sweetened condensed milk into a heatproof bowl or jar.
2. Cover the bowl or jar tightly with aluminum foil or a lid.
3. Place the bowl or jar in a larger pot or saucepan and fill the pot with enough water to completely submerge the bowl or jar.
4. Bring the water to a simmer over medium heat.
5. Reduce the heat to low and let the sweetened condensed milk simmer gently for 2-3 hours, stirring occasionally, or until it thickens and turns into a caramel-like consistency.
6. Check the water level periodically and add more water as needed to keep the bowl or jar submerged.
7. Once the sweetened condensed milk has reached the desired consistency and color, remove it from the pot and let it cool to room temperature.
8. Once cooled, transfer the Dulce de Leche to an airtight container and store it in the refrigerator until ready to use.

Enjoy this delicious and versatile Dulce de Leche as a spread on toast, filling for cakes and pastries, topping for ice cream, or simply eaten by the spoonful! It adds a rich and indulgent sweetness to any dessert.

Golfeados

Dough Ingredients:

- 4 cups all-purpose flour
- 1/4 cup granulated sugar
- 1 teaspoon salt
- 1/2 cup unsalted butter, melted
- 1 cup warm milk
- 2 teaspoons active dry yeast
- 2 large eggs

Filling Ingredients:

- 1 cup grated queso de mano or mozzarella cheese
- 1/4 cup unsalted butter, softened
- 1/4 cup granulated sugar
- 1 teaspoon ground cinnamon

Syrup Ingredients:

- 1 cup panela or brown sugar
- 1/2 cup water
- 1 cinnamon stick

Instructions:

Dough:

1. In a small bowl, dissolve the yeast in warm milk and let it sit for about 5 minutes until frothy.
2. In a large mixing bowl, combine the flour, sugar, and salt.
3. Add the melted butter, yeast mixture, and eggs to the dry ingredients. Mix until a dough forms.
4. Knead the dough on a floured surface for about 5-7 minutes until smooth and elastic.
5. Place the dough in a greased bowl, cover with a clean kitchen towel, and let it rise in a warm place for about 1-2 hours, or until doubled in size.

Filling:

1. In a small bowl, mix together the softened butter, granulated sugar, and ground cinnamon until well combined.
2. Punch down the risen dough and roll it out into a rectangle on a floured surface.
3. Spread the butter-sugar mixture evenly over the surface of the dough.
4. Sprinkle the grated cheese evenly over the butter-sugar mixture.

Assembly:

1. Roll up the dough tightly from one long edge to form a log.
2. Cut the log into 12 equal-sized pieces.
3. Place the rolls, cut side down, in a greased baking dish, leaving space between each roll.
4. Cover the baking dish with a clean kitchen towel and let the rolls rise for another 30-45 minutes, or until puffed up.

Syrup:

1. In a small saucepan, combine the panela (or brown sugar), water, and cinnamon stick.
2. Bring the mixture to a simmer over medium heat, stirring occasionally, until the sugar is dissolved and the syrup thickens slightly.
3. Remove the cinnamon stick and set the syrup aside to cool slightly.

Baking:

1. Preheat your oven to 350°F (175°C).
2. Bake the golfeados in the preheated oven for 20-25 minutes, or until golden brown.
3. Remove the golfeados from the oven and pour the syrup over them while they are still warm.
4. Let the golfeados cool slightly before serving.

Enjoy these delicious Golfeados as a sweet and indulgent treat, perfect for breakfast or as a snack with coffee or tea!

Tizana

Ingredients:

- Assorted fresh fruits, such as:
    - Pineapple, diced
    - Watermelon, diced
    - Cantaloupe or honeydew melon, diced
    - Mango, diced
    - Papaya, diced
    - Oranges, segmented
    - Strawberries, sliced
    - Grapes, halved
    - Kiwi, peeled and diced
- Fruit juice, such as:
    - Orange juice
    - Pineapple juice
    - Mango juice
- Sugar or honey, to taste
- Ice cubes
- Fresh mint leaves, for garnish (optional)

Instructions:

1. Wash and prepare the assorted fresh fruits by dicing or slicing them as desired. You can use any combination of fruits you like, depending on availability and personal preference.
2. In a large pitcher or bowl, combine the prepared fruits.
3. Pour the fruit juices over the mixed fruits, using a ratio that suits your taste preferences. You can use equal parts of each juice or adjust the proportions according to your preference.
4. Sweeten the Tizana with sugar or honey, if desired, stirring until the sweetener is dissolved. Start with a small amount and adjust to taste.
5. Add ice cubes to the pitcher or individual serving glasses to chill the Tizana.
6. Stir the Tizana gently to combine all the ingredients.
7. Garnish the Tizana with fresh mint leaves, if desired, for a burst of freshness.
8. Serve the Tizana immediately as a refreshing drink on a hot day.

Enjoy this vibrant and delicious Tizana filled with a variety of fresh fruits, perfect for cooling down and hydrating during warm weather! Feel free to customize the fruits and juices according to your preferences and what's in season.

Cazón en Salsa

Ingredients:

- 1 pound shark fillets, cut into bite-sized pieces
- 2 tablespoons lime or lemon juice
- Salt and pepper, to taste
- 2 tablespoons vegetable oil
- 1 onion, finely chopped
- 2 cloves garlic, minced
- 1 bell pepper, diced
- 2 tomatoes, diced
- 1 cup fish or vegetable broth
- 1 teaspoon ground cumin
- 1 teaspoon dried oregano
- 1/2 teaspoon paprika
- 1/4 teaspoon cayenne pepper (optional, for heat)
- 2 bay leaves
- Fresh cilantro or parsley, chopped, for garnish

Instructions:

1. Place the shark fillets in a bowl and season them with lime or lemon juice, salt, and pepper. Let them marinate for about 15-20 minutes.
2. In a large skillet or saucepan, heat the vegetable oil over medium heat. Add the chopped onion, minced garlic, and diced bell pepper, and sauté until softened.
3. Add the diced tomatoes to the skillet and cook until they start to soften and release their juices.
4. Stir in the fish or vegetable broth, ground cumin, dried oregano, paprika, cayenne pepper (if using), and bay leaves. Bring the mixture to a simmer.
5. Add the marinated shark fillets to the skillet, along with any accumulated juices. Cover the skillet and let the cazón simmer gently for about 10-15 minutes, or until the fish is cooked through and tender.
6. Once the fish is cooked, remove the bay leaves from the skillet and discard them.
7. Taste the sauce and adjust the seasoning with salt and pepper, if needed.
8. Serve the Cazón en Salsa hot, garnished with chopped fresh cilantro or parsley.

Enjoy this flavorful and comforting Cazón en Salsa as a delicious main course, served with rice, plantains, or arepas for a complete meal!

Pabellón Oriental

Ingredients:

- 1 pound flank steak or skirt steak, thinly sliced
- 1 onion, chopped
- 2 cloves garlic, minced
- 1 red bell pepper, thinly sliced
- 1 green bell pepper, thinly sliced
- 2 tomatoes, diced
- 1 tablespoon soy sauce
- 1 tablespoon Worcestershire sauce
- 1 teaspoon ground cumin
- 1/2 teaspoon paprika
- Salt and pepper, to taste
- Vegetable oil, for cooking
- Cooked white rice, for serving
- Cooked black beans, for serving
- Ripe plantains, sliced and fried, for serving
- Fresh cilantro or parsley, chopped, for garnish

Instructions:

1. In a large skillet or frying pan, heat some vegetable oil over medium-high heat. Add the thinly sliced steak and cook until browned on both sides. Remove the steak from the skillet and set aside.
2. In the same skillet, add a little more vegetable oil if needed. Add the chopped onion and minced garlic, and sauté until softened and fragrant.
3. Add the sliced red and green bell peppers to the skillet and cook until they start to soften.
4. Stir in the diced tomatoes, soy sauce, Worcestershire sauce, ground cumin, paprika, salt, and pepper. Cook for a few minutes until the tomatoes break down and the mixture becomes saucy.
5. Return the cooked steak to the skillet and toss it with the vegetable mixture until heated through and well coated with the sauce.
6. Taste and adjust the seasoning with salt and pepper, if needed.
7. Serve the Pabellón Oriental hot, accompanied by cooked white rice, black beans, and sliced fried plantains.
8. Garnish with chopped fresh cilantro or parsley before serving.

Enjoy this delicious and flavorful Pabellón Oriental as a satisfying meal, combining the richness of beef with the aromatic Eastern spices, served alongside classic Venezuelan accompaniments!

Arroz con Leche

Ingredients:

- 1 cup white rice
- 4 cups whole milk
- 1 cinnamon stick
- 1/2 cup granulated sugar (adjust to taste)
- 1 teaspoon vanilla extract
- Ground cinnamon, for garnish (optional)
- Raisins, for garnish (optional)

Instructions:

1. Rinse the white rice under cold water until the water runs clear. Drain well.
2. In a large saucepan, combine the rinsed rice, whole milk, and cinnamon stick.
3. Bring the mixture to a gentle boil over medium heat, stirring occasionally to prevent the rice from sticking to the bottom of the pan.
4. Once the mixture comes to a boil, reduce the heat to low and simmer, uncovered, stirring frequently, for about 30-40 minutes, or until the rice is tender and the mixture has thickened to a creamy consistency.
5. Stir in the granulated sugar and vanilla extract, and continue to cook for another 5-10 minutes, stirring constantly, until the sugar is dissolved and the rice pudding is creamy and smooth.
6. Remove the cinnamon stick from the rice pudding and discard it.
7. Remove the rice pudding from the heat and let it cool slightly.
8. Transfer the rice pudding to serving bowls or a large serving dish.
9. Serve the Arroz con Leche warm or chilled, garnished with a sprinkle of ground cinnamon and raisins, if desired.

Enjoy this creamy and comforting Arroz con Leche as a delicious dessert or snack, perfect for satisfying your sweet cravings! Adjust the sweetness and consistency according to your taste preferences.

Chivo en Coco

Ingredients:

- 2 pounds goat meat, cut into cubes
- 1 onion, chopped
- 3 cloves garlic, minced
- 1 red bell pepper, diced
- 1 green bell pepper, diced
- 2 tomatoes, diced
- 2 cups coconut milk
- 1 cup water or beef broth
- 2 tablespoons vegetable oil
- 2 tablespoons tomato paste
- 1 tablespoon ground cumin
- 1 tablespoon ground coriander
- 1 teaspoon ground turmeric
- Salt and pepper, to taste
- Fresh cilantro, chopped, for garnish

Instructions:

1. In a large pot or Dutch oven, heat the vegetable oil over medium heat. Add the chopped onion and minced garlic, and sauté until softened and fragrant.
2. Add the diced red and green bell peppers to the pot and cook until they start to soften.
3. Stir in the diced tomatoes and tomato paste, and cook for a few minutes until the tomatoes break down.
4. Add the cubed goat meat to the pot and season with ground cumin, ground coriander, ground turmeric, salt, and pepper. Cook until the meat is browned on all sides.
5. Pour in the coconut milk and water or beef broth, and stir to combine.
6. Bring the mixture to a simmer, then reduce the heat to low. Cover the pot and let the Chivo en Coco simmer gently for about 2-3 hours, or until the goat meat is tender and the sauce has thickened.
7. Taste and adjust the seasoning with salt and pepper, if needed.
8. Once the goat meat is tender and the sauce has reached the desired consistency, remove the pot from the heat.
9. Serve the Chivo en Coco hot, garnished with chopped fresh cilantro.

Enjoy this flavorful and aromatic Chivo en Coco with rice, plantains, or arepas for a satisfying and comforting meal that's sure to impress!

Tequenos de Hojaldre

Ingredients:

- 1 sheet of puff pastry, thawed according to package instructions
- 200 grams (about 7 ounces) of queso blanco or mozzarella cheese, cut into sticks
- 1 egg, beaten (for egg wash)
- Vegetable oil, for frying

Instructions:

1. Preheat your oven to 375°F (190°C).
2. On a lightly floured surface, roll out the puff pastry sheet into a rectangle that's about 1/8 inch thick.
3. Using a sharp knife or pizza cutter, cut the puff pastry into strips that are about 1 inch wide and 4 inches long.
4. Place a stick of cheese at one end of each puff pastry strip, leaving a small border.
5. Roll up the puff pastry tightly around the cheese stick, pressing gently to seal the edges.
6. Repeat with the remaining puff pastry strips and cheese sticks.
7. Place the rolled Tequeños de Hojaldre on a baking sheet lined with parchment paper.
8. Brush the tops of the Tequeños with beaten egg to give them a golden color when baked.
9. Bake in the preheated oven for about 15-20 minutes, or until the Tequeños are puffed and golden brown.
10. Remove the Tequeños from the oven and let them cool slightly.

To fry:

1. Heat vegetable oil in a deep fryer or large skillet to 350°F (175°C).
2. Carefully add the Tequeños to the hot oil in batches, making sure not to overcrowd the pan.
3. Fry the Tequeños for about 2-3 minutes, or until they are golden brown and crispy.
4. Remove the fried Tequeños from the oil using a slotted spoon and drain them on paper towels to remove excess oil.

5. Serve the Tequeños de Hojaldre hot with your favorite dipping sauce, such as salsa rosada, guasacaca, or ketchup.

Enjoy these crispy and cheesy Tequeños de Hojaldre as a delicious appetizer or snack for any occasion!

Torta de Piña

Ingredients:

- 1/4 cup unsalted butter
- 3/4 cup brown sugar, packed
- 1 can (20 ounces) pineapple slices, drained
- Maraschino cherries, drained
- 1 1/2 cups all-purpose flour
- 1 1/2 teaspoons baking powder
- 1/4 teaspoon salt
- 1/2 cup unsalted butter, softened
- 3/4 cup granulated sugar
- 2 large eggs
- 1 teaspoon vanilla extract
- 1/2 cup milk

Instructions:

1. Preheat your oven to 350°F (175°C). Grease a 9-inch round cake pan and line the bottom with parchment paper.
2. In a small saucepan, melt 1/4 cup of unsalted butter over medium heat. Stir in the brown sugar until it's dissolved and well combined.
3. Pour the melted butter and brown sugar mixture into the prepared cake pan, spreading it evenly across the bottom.
4. Arrange the pineapple slices on top of the caramelized sugar in the cake pan. Place a maraschino cherry in the center of each pineapple slice and in between them as desired.
5. In a medium mixing bowl, sift together the all-purpose flour, baking powder, and salt.
6. In a separate large mixing bowl, cream together the softened unsalted butter and granulated sugar until light and fluffy.
7. Beat in the eggs, one at a time, until well combined. Stir in the vanilla extract.
8. Gradually add the dry ingredients to the wet ingredients, alternating with the milk, and mix until just combined. Be careful not to overmix.
9. Pour the cake batter over the pineapple slices in the cake pan, spreading it evenly.
10. Bake in the preheated oven for 40-45 minutes, or until a toothpick inserted into the center of the cake comes out clean.

11. Remove the cake from the oven and let it cool in the pan for about 10 minutes.
12. Carefully invert the cake onto a serving plate or cake stand while it's still warm. Remove the parchment paper from the top.
13. Allow the cake to cool completely before slicing and serving.

Enjoy this classic Torta de Piña with its caramelized pineapple topping for a delightful dessert that's perfect for any occasion!

Ceviche de Camarones

Ingredients:

- 1 pound medium shrimp, peeled and deveined
- 1 cup fresh lime juice (about 8-10 limes)
- 1 small red onion, thinly sliced
- 1 tomato, diced
- 1/2 cup chopped fresh cilantro
- 1 jalapeño or serrano pepper, seeded and finely chopped (optional)
- Salt, to taste
- Pepper, to taste
- Avocado slices, for garnish (optional)
- Tortilla chips or tostadas, for serving

Instructions:

1. Bring a large pot of salted water to a boil. Add the shrimp and cook for 1-2 minutes, or until they turn pink and opaque. Be careful not to overcook them.
2. Drain the cooked shrimp and transfer them to a large bowl.
3. Add the fresh lime juice to the bowl with the shrimp, making sure they are fully submerged. Let the shrimp marinate in the lime juice for about 10-15 minutes. The acid from the lime juice will "cook" the shrimp and give them a firm texture.
4. While the shrimp are marinating, prepare the other ingredients. Thinly slice the red onion, dice the tomato, chop the fresh cilantro, and finely chop the jalapeño or serrano pepper (if using).
5. After the shrimp have marinated, drain off most of the lime juice, leaving just enough to keep the shrimp moist.
6. Add the sliced red onion, diced tomato, chopped cilantro, and chopped jalapeño or serrano pepper to the bowl with the shrimp.
7. Season the ceviche with salt and pepper, to taste. Gently toss everything together until well combined.
8. Cover the bowl with plastic wrap and refrigerate the ceviche for at least 30 minutes to allow the flavors to meld together.
9. When ready to serve, give the ceviche a final stir and taste for seasoning, adjusting as needed.
10. Serve the Ceviche de Camarones chilled, garnished with avocado slices if desired, alongside tortilla chips or tostadas for scooping.

Enjoy this refreshing and zesty Ceviche de Camarones as a light and satisfying appetizer or snack, perfect for a hot summer day or any occasion!

Pata e' Vaca

Ingredients:

- 2 cow's feet, cleaned and cut into pieces
- 1 onion, chopped
- 3 cloves garlic, minced
- 2 carrots, peeled and diced
- 2 potatoes, peeled and diced
- 1 bell pepper, chopped
- 2 tomatoes, diced
- 1 tablespoon vegetable oil
- 1 tablespoon tomato paste
- 1 teaspoon ground cumin
- 1 teaspoon dried oregano
- Salt and pepper, to taste
- Water or beef broth
- Fresh cilantro or parsley, chopped, for garnish

Instructions:

1. In a large pot or Dutch oven, heat the vegetable oil over medium heat. Add the chopped onion and minced garlic, and sauté until softened and fragrant.
2. Add the cow's feet pieces to the pot and brown them on all sides.
3. Stir in the diced carrots, potatoes, bell pepper, and tomatoes.
4. Add enough water or beef broth to cover the ingredients in the pot. Bring the mixture to a boil.
5. Reduce the heat to low, cover the pot, and let the stew simmer gently for about 2-3 hours, or until the cow's feet are tender and the vegetables are cooked through.
6. Stir in the tomato paste, ground cumin, dried oregano, salt, and pepper. Adjust the seasoning to taste.
7. Continue to simmer the stew uncovered for another 15-20 minutes to allow the flavors to meld together and the sauce to thicken slightly.
8. Once the stew is ready, remove it from the heat and let it cool slightly.
9. Serve the Pata e' Vaca hot, garnished with chopped fresh cilantro or parsley.

Enjoy this hearty and comforting Pata e' Vaca stew as a satisfying meal, accompanied by rice, arepas, or crusty bread for soaking up the flavorful sauce!

Teta e' Monja

Ingredients:

- 1 cow's udder, cleaned and sliced into pieces
- 1 onion, chopped
- 3 cloves garlic, minced
- 2 carrots, peeled and diced
- 2 potatoes, peeled and diced
- 1 bell pepper, chopped
- 2 tomatoes, diced
- 1 tablespoon vegetable oil
- 1 tablespoon tomato paste
- 1 teaspoon ground cumin
- 1 teaspoon dried oregano
- Salt and pepper, to taste
- Water or beef broth
- Fresh cilantro or parsley, chopped, for garnish

Instructions:

1. In a large pot or Dutch oven, heat the vegetable oil over medium heat. Add the chopped onion and minced garlic, and sauté until softened and fragrant.
2. Add the sliced cow's udder pieces to the pot and brown them on all sides.
3. Stir in the diced carrots, potatoes, bell pepper, and tomatoes.
4. Add enough water or beef broth to cover the ingredients in the pot. Bring the mixture to a boil.
5. Reduce the heat to low, cover the pot, and let the stew simmer gently for about 2-3 hours, or until the cow's udder is tender and the vegetables are cooked through.
6. Stir in the tomato paste, ground cumin, dried oregano, salt, and pepper. Adjust the seasoning to taste.
7. Continue to simmer the stew uncovered for another 15-20 minutes to allow the flavors to meld together and the sauce to thicken slightly.
8. Once the stew is ready, remove it from the heat and let it cool slightly.
9. Serve the Teta e' Monja hot, garnished with chopped fresh cilantro or parsley.

Please note that cow's udder may not be readily available or commonly consumed in many places outside of Venezuela, and some people may find the concept unfamiliar or unappealing. As with any unconventional dish, it's important to source the ingredients from reputable sources and ensure they are properly cleaned and prepared before cooking.

Mandoca de Platano

Ingredients:

- 3 ripe plantains, peeled and mashed
- 1 cup pre-cooked cornmeal (masarepa or harina precocida)
- 1/4 cup granulated sugar
- 1/4 teaspoon salt
- 1/4 teaspoon ground cinnamon (optional)
- Vegetable oil, for frying

Instructions:

1. In a large mixing bowl, combine the mashed ripe plantains, pre-cooked cornmeal, granulated sugar, salt, and ground cinnamon (if using). Mix well until a dough forms.
2. Heat vegetable oil in a deep fryer or large skillet to 350°F (175°C).
3. Take a small portion of the dough and shape it into a ball or disk about 2-3 inches in diameter and 1/2 inch thick. Repeat with the remaining dough.
4. Carefully add the shaped mandocas to the hot oil in batches, making sure not to overcrowd the pan.
5. Fry the mandocas for about 3-4 minutes on each side, or until they are golden brown and crispy.
6. Remove the fried mandocas from the oil using a slotted spoon and drain them on paper towels to remove excess oil.
7. Serve the Mandoca de Plátano warm.

Enjoy these delicious Mandocas de Plátano as a tasty snack or breakfast treat, either on their own or with a cup of hot chocolate or coffee! Feel free to adjust the sweetness and seasoning according to your taste preferences.

Asopado de Mariscos

Ingredients:

- 1 pound mixed seafood (shrimp, mussels, squid, scallops, etc.), cleaned and deveined
- 1 cup long-grain white rice
- 1 onion, finely chopped
- 3 cloves garlic, minced
- 1 bell pepper, diced
- 2 tomatoes, diced
- 1/4 cup chopped cilantro or parsley
- 6 cups fish or seafood broth
- 2 tablespoons tomato paste
- 1 teaspoon ground cumin
- 1 teaspoon paprika
- Salt and pepper, to taste
- Olive oil, for cooking
- Lime wedges, for serving
- Additional chopped cilantro or parsley, for garnish

Instructions:

1. In a large pot or Dutch oven, heat a drizzle of olive oil over medium heat. Add the chopped onion and minced garlic, and sauté until softened and fragrant.
2. Add the diced bell pepper and tomatoes to the pot, and cook until they start to soften.
3. Stir in the tomato paste, ground cumin, paprika, salt, and pepper. Cook for a few minutes to allow the flavors to meld together.
4. Add the long-grain white rice to the pot, and stir to coat it with the onion and tomato mixture.
5. Pour in the fish or seafood broth, and bring the mixture to a boil.
6. Reduce the heat to low, cover the pot, and let the soup simmer for about 15-20 minutes, or until the rice is cooked through and tender.
7. Once the rice is cooked, add the mixed seafood to the pot, and stir to combine.
8. Let the soup simmer for an additional 5-7 minutes, or until the seafood is cooked through. Be careful not to overcook the seafood, as it can become tough.
9. Stir in the chopped cilantro or parsley, and taste the soup for seasoning, adjusting as needed with salt and pepper.

10. Serve the Asopado de Mariscos hot, garnished with additional chopped cilantro or parsley, and lime wedges on the side.

Enjoy this delicious and comforting Asopado de Mariscos as a satisfying meal, perfect for warming up on a chilly day or enjoying with family and friends!

Chicha Andina

Ingredients:

- 2 cups dried maize (maíz morado or purple corn is traditional, but you can use other varieties)
- 10 cups water
- 1 cinnamon stick
- 4 cloves
- 1 cup sugar (adjust to taste)
- Pineapple or apple peels (optional, for added flavor)

Instructions:

1. Rinse the dried maize under cold water to remove any debris.
2. In a large pot, combine the dried maize and water. Add the cinnamon stick, cloves, and pineapple or apple peels (if using).
3. Bring the mixture to a boil over high heat, then reduce the heat to low and let it simmer uncovered for about 1-2 hours, stirring occasionally.
4. After simmering, remove the pot from the heat and let the mixture cool to room temperature.
5. Once the mixture has cooled, strain it through a fine mesh sieve or cheesecloth into a clean container to remove the solids. Press down on the solids to extract as much liquid as possible.
6. Stir in the sugar until dissolved, adjusting the sweetness to your taste.
7. Transfer the strained liquid to a large pitcher or individual serving glasses.
8. Chill the Chicha Andina in the refrigerator for at least a few hours before serving.
9. Serve the Chicha Andina cold, optionally garnishing with additional cinnamon sticks or fruit slices.

Enjoy this refreshing and lightly sweetened Chicha Andina as a traditional Andean beverage, perfect for hot days or special occasions! Adjust the flavorings and sweetness to suit your preferences.

Hallaca Andina

Ingredients:

For the Filling:

- 1 pound pork shoulder, diced
- 1 pound beef chuck, diced
- 1 pound chicken breast, diced
- 2 onions, finely chopped
- 4 cloves garlic, minced
- 1 bell pepper, finely chopped
- 2 tomatoes, diced
- 1/2 cup raisins
- 1/2 cup pitted green olives, sliced
- 1/2 cup capers
- 1/2 cup cooked chickpeas
- 1/2 cup cooked black beans
- 1/4 cup vegetable oil
- 1/4 cup white wine
- 1/4 cup Worcestershire sauce
- 1/4 cup soy sauce
- 1/4 cup tomato paste
- 1 teaspoon ground cumin
- 1 teaspoon dried oregano
- Salt and pepper, to taste

For the Dough:

- 3 cups pre-cooked cornmeal (masarepa or harina precocida)
- 4 cups chicken or vegetable broth
- 1/2 cup vegetable oil
- Salt, to taste

For Assembly:

- Plantain leaves, cleaned and cut into rectangles
- Kitchen twine or toothpicks

Instructions:

For the Filling:

1. In a large skillet or Dutch oven, heat the vegetable oil over medium heat. Add the diced pork, beef, and chicken, and cook until browned on all sides. Remove from the skillet and set aside.
2. In the same skillet, add the chopped onions, minced garlic, and chopped bell pepper. Sauté until softened.
3. Stir in the diced tomatoes, raisins, sliced olives, capers, cooked chickpeas, cooked black beans, white wine, Worcestershire sauce, soy sauce, tomato paste, ground cumin, dried oregano, salt, and pepper. Cook for a few minutes until the flavors meld together.
4. Return the browned meats to the skillet and mix well with the vegetable mixture. Cook for an additional 10-15 minutes, stirring occasionally, until the filling is thick and flavorful. Remove from heat and let it cool.

For the Dough:

1. In a large mixing bowl, combine the pre-cooked cornmeal and chicken or vegetable broth. Mix well until a soft dough forms.
2. Stir in the vegetable oil and salt, kneading the dough until smooth and pliable.

For Assembly:

1. Lay out a piece of plantain leaf and spread a portion of the dough on top, shaping it into a rectangle.
2. Place a generous spoonful of the filling in the center of the dough rectangle.
3. Fold the sides of the plantain leaf over the filling to enclose it completely, then fold the top and bottom edges to seal the hallaca.
4. Secure the hallaca with kitchen twine or toothpicks.
5. Repeat the process with the remaining dough and filling.

6. Steam the hallacas in a large pot or steamer for about 1-2 hours, or until the dough is cooked through and firm.
7. Remove the hallacas from the steamer and let them cool slightly before serving.

Enjoy these delicious and flavorful Hallacas Andinas as a traditional Venezuelan dish, perfect for special occasions or holiday celebrations! Adjust the filling ingredients and seasonings to suit your taste preferences.

Cocada

Ingredients:

- 4 cups shredded coconut (fresh or dried)
- 2 cups granulated sugar
- 1 cup water
- 1 teaspoon vanilla extract (optional)
- Pinch of salt (optional)

Instructions:

1. In a large skillet or saucepan, combine the granulated sugar and water over medium heat, stirring until the sugar is dissolved.
2. Add the shredded coconut to the saucepan and stir to combine.
3. Continue to cook the mixture over medium heat, stirring frequently, until it thickens and most of the liquid has evaporated, about 10-15 minutes.
4. If using, stir in the vanilla extract and a pinch of salt to enhance the flavor.
5. Once the mixture has thickened to your desired consistency and the coconut is evenly coated with the sugar syrup, remove the saucepan from the heat.
6. Line a baking sheet or tray with parchment paper or greased foil.
7. Using a spoon or cookie scoop, drop small mounds of the coconut mixture onto the prepared baking sheet, spacing them apart to allow room for spreading.
8. Let the Cocadas cool and set at room temperature for about 1-2 hours, or until firm.
9. Once the Cocadas have cooled and set, you can store them in an airtight container at room temperature for several days.

Enjoy these delicious Cocadas as a sweet treat or dessert, perfect for satisfying your coconut cravings! Feel free to customize the recipe by adding nuts, chocolate chips, or other flavorings to suit your taste preferences.

Tigrillo

Ingredients:

- 4 green (unripe) plantains, peeled and roughly chopped
- 4 eggs
- 1 onion, finely chopped
- 2 tomatoes, diced
- 2 tablespoons vegetable oil
- 1/2 cup queso fresco or feta cheese, crumbled
- Salt and pepper, to taste
- Fresh cilantro or parsley, chopped, for garnish (optional)

Instructions:

1. Place the chopped green plantains in a pot of boiling water and cook until tender, about 15-20 minutes.
2. Drain the cooked plantains and transfer them to a large mixing bowl.
3. Mash the cooked plantains using a potato masher or fork until smooth and lump-free. Set aside.
4. In a large skillet, heat the vegetable oil over medium heat. Add the finely chopped onion and cook until translucent.
5. Add the diced tomatoes to the skillet and cook until softened.
6. Crack the eggs into the skillet and scramble them with the onions and tomatoes until cooked through.
7. Add the mashed green plantains to the skillet and mix everything together until well combined.
8. Cook the mixture for a few more minutes, stirring occasionally, until heated through.
9. Stir in the crumbled queso fresco or feta cheese, and season with salt and pepper to taste.
10. Once everything is well combined and heated through, remove the skillet from the heat.
11. Serve the Tigrillo hot, garnished with chopped fresh cilantro or parsley if desired.

Enjoy this delicious and hearty Tigrillo as a traditional Ecuadorian breakfast or brunch dish, perfect for starting your day with a burst of flavor and energy! Feel free to customize the recipe by adding additional ingredients such as cooked bacon, sausage, or avocado slices to suit your taste preferences.

Llanero

Ingredients:

- 2 pounds beef sirloin or flank steak, cut into 1-inch cubes
- 1 onion, finely chopped
- 4 cloves garlic, minced
- 1/4 cup Worcestershire sauce
- 1/4 cup soy sauce
- 2 tablespoons vegetable oil
- 1 tablespoon ground cumin
- 1 tablespoon paprika
- Salt and pepper, to taste
- Wooden skewers, soaked in water for at least 30 minutes

Instructions:

1. In a large mixing bowl, combine the chopped onion, minced garlic, Worcestershire sauce, soy sauce, vegetable oil, ground cumin, paprika, salt, and pepper. Mix well to combine.
2. Add the cubed beef to the marinade, making sure each piece is well coated. Cover the bowl and let the beef marinate in the refrigerator for at least 1-2 hours, or preferably overnight, to allow the flavors to meld together.
3. When ready to cook, preheat your grill or barbecue to medium-high heat.
4. Thread the marinated beef cubes onto the soaked wooden skewers, leaving a little space between each piece.
5. Place the skewers on the preheated grill and cook for about 3-4 minutes per side, or until the beef is cooked to your desired level of doneness and has nice grill marks.
6. Remove the skewers from the grill and let them rest for a few minutes before serving.
7. Serve the Carne en Vara hot, garnished with chopped fresh cilantro or parsley if desired.

Enjoy these delicious Carne en Vara skewers as a classic llanero dish, perfect for grilling outdoors and enjoying with friends and family! Pair them with traditional llanero sides like arepas, yuca, or grilled vegetables for a complete meal.

Bistec a Caballo

Ingredients:

- 4 beef steaks (such as sirloin or ribeye), about 1/2 inch thick
- Salt and pepper, to taste
- 4 eggs
- Vegetable oil, for frying
- Cooked white rice, for serving
- Cooked black beans, for serving
- Fried ripe plantains (plátanos maduros), for serving
- Chopped fresh cilantro or parsley, for garnish (optional)

Instructions:

1. Season the beef steaks generously with salt and pepper on both sides.
2. Heat a grill or grill pan over medium-high heat. Alternatively, you can cook the steaks in a skillet on the stovetop.
3. Grill or pan-fry the steaks for about 3-4 minutes per side, or until they reach your desired level of doneness. Remove them from the heat and let them rest while you prepare the eggs.
4. In a separate skillet, heat a little vegetable oil over medium heat. Crack the eggs into the skillet and fry them until the whites are set and the yolks are still slightly runny, or to your desired level of doneness.
5. To serve, place a cooked steak on each plate and top each steak with a fried egg.
6. Serve the Bistec a Caballo with cooked white rice, black beans, and fried ripe plantains on the side.
7. Garnish with chopped fresh cilantro or parsley, if desired.

Enjoy this hearty and satisfying Bistec a Caballo as a classic Colombian dish, perfect for lunch or dinner! Adjust the seasonings and accompaniments to suit your taste preferences.

Guasacaca

Ingredients:

- 2 ripe avocados, peeled and pitted
- 1/2 cup chopped fresh cilantro
- 1/4 cup chopped fresh parsley
- 1/4 cup chopped green bell pepper
- 1/4 cup chopped onion
- 2 cloves garlic, minced
- 2 tablespoons white vinegar
- Juice of 1 lime
- 1/4 cup olive oil
- Salt and pepper, to taste
- Hot sauce or chopped jalapeño (optional, for heat)

Instructions:

1. In a food processor or blender, combine the ripe avocados, chopped cilantro, chopped parsley, chopped green bell pepper, chopped onion, minced garlic, white vinegar, lime juice, and olive oil.
2. Blend the ingredients until smooth and well combined. If the sauce is too thick, you can add a little water to thin it out to your desired consistency.
3. Season the Guasacaca with salt and pepper to taste. If you like spicy food, you can also add hot sauce or chopped jalapeño for some heat.
4. Transfer the Guasacaca to a serving bowl or container and refrigerate for at least 30 minutes to allow the flavors to meld together.
5. Serve the Guasacaca chilled as a condiment or dipping sauce alongside grilled meats, arepas, empanadas, or other dishes.

Enjoy this delicious and versatile Guasacaca sauce as a flavorful accompaniment to your favorite Venezuelan dishes! Feel free to adjust the ingredients and seasonings to suit your taste preferences.

Mandoca de Yuca

Ingredients:

- 2 cups yuca (cassava) flour
- 1/2 cup granulated sugar
- 1/2 teaspoon salt
- 1/2 teaspoon ground cinnamon (optional)
- 1/4 teaspoon ground nutmeg (optional)
- 1/4 cup unsalted butter, melted
- 1/4 cup milk
- Vegetable oil, for frying

Instructions:

1. In a large mixing bowl, combine the yuca flour, granulated sugar, salt, ground cinnamon, and ground nutmeg. Mix well to combine.
2. Add the melted unsalted butter and milk to the dry ingredients. Mix until a dough forms. If the dough is too dry, you can add a little more milk, one tablespoon at a time, until the dough comes together.
3. Divide the dough into small portions and shape each portion into a ball or disk, about 2-3 inches in diameter and 1/2 inch thick. You can also shape the dough into small logs or other desired shapes.
4. Heat vegetable oil in a deep fryer or large skillet to 350°F (175°C).
5. Carefully add the shaped Mandoca de Yuca to the hot oil in batches, making sure not to overcrowd the pan.
6. Fry the Mandoca de Yuca for about 3-4 minutes on each side, or until they are golden brown and crispy.
7. Remove the fried Mandoca de Yuca from the oil using a slotted spoon and drain them on paper towels to remove excess oil.
8. Serve the Mandoca de Yuca warm, optionally topped with cheese, butter, or other desired toppings.

Enjoy these delicious Mandoca de Yuca fritters as a tasty snack or breakfast treat, perfect for enjoying with a cup of coffee or tea! Feel free to adjust the sweetness and seasonings to suit your taste preferences.

Pastelitos de Chucho

Ingredients:

- 1 pound chucho fish fillets, cooked and shredded
- 2 tablespoons vegetable oil
- 1 onion, finely chopped
- 2 cloves garlic, minced
- 1 bell pepper, finely chopped
- 2 tomatoes, diced
- 1/4 cup chopped fresh cilantro
- 1/4 cup chopped green olives
- 1/4 cup capers
- 1 teaspoon ground cumin
- 1 teaspoon paprika
- Salt and pepper, to taste
- Prepared empanada dough or puff pastry sheets
- Vegetable oil, for frying (if using empanada dough)

Instructions:

1. Heat vegetable oil in a skillet over medium heat. Add the chopped onion, minced garlic, and bell pepper. Cook until softened, about 5 minutes.
2. Add the diced tomatoes to the skillet and cook until they start to break down, about 5-7 minutes.
3. Stir in the shredded chucho fish, chopped cilantro, green olives, capers, ground cumin, paprika, salt, and pepper. Cook for another 5 minutes, stirring occasionally, until the mixture is well combined and heated through.
4. Remove the skillet from the heat and let the filling cool slightly.
5. Roll out the prepared empanada dough or puff pastry sheets on a lightly floured surface. Cut the dough into circles using a round cutter or the rim of a glass.
6. Place a spoonful of the chucho fish filling in the center of each dough circle. Fold the dough over the filling to form a half-moon shape, then seal the edges by pressing with a fork.
7. Heat vegetable oil in a deep fryer or large skillet to 350°F (175°C). Carefully add the pastelitos to the hot oil in batches and fry until golden brown and crispy, about 3-4 minutes per side.
8. Remove the pastelitos from the oil and drain them on paper towels to remove excess oil.

9. Serve the pastelitos de chucho hot, optionally with a side of tartar sauce or hot sauce for dipping.

Enjoy these delicious pastelitos de chucho as a tasty appetizer or snack, perfect for enjoying with family and friends! Adjust the seasonings and add additional ingredients according to your taste preferences.

Hallaca Oriental

Ingredients:

For the Dough:

- 3 cups pre-cooked cornmeal (masarepa or harina precocida)
- 4 cups chicken or vegetable broth
- 1/2 cup vegetable oil
- Salt, to taste

For the Filling:

- 1 pound pork shoulder, diced
- 1 pound beef chuck, diced
- 1 pound chicken breast, diced
- 1 onion, finely chopped
- 4 cloves garlic, minced
- 1 bell pepper, finely chopped
- 2 tomatoes, diced
- 1/2 cup raisins
- 1/2 cup pitted green olives, sliced
- 1/2 cup capers
- 1/4 cup vegetable oil
- 1/4 cup white wine
- 1/4 cup Worcestershire sauce
- 1/4 cup soy sauce
- 1/4 cup tomato paste
- 1 teaspoon ground cumin
- 1 teaspoon paprika
- Salt and pepper, to taste

For Assembly:

- Plantain leaves, cleaned and cut into rectangles
- Kitchen twine or toothpicks

Instructions:

1. Prepare the dough: In a large mixing bowl, combine the pre-cooked cornmeal and chicken or vegetable broth. Mix well until a soft dough forms. Stir in the vegetable oil and salt, kneading the dough until smooth and pliable.
2. Prepare the filling: In a large skillet or Dutch oven, heat the vegetable oil over medium heat. Add the diced pork, beef, and chicken, and cook until browned on all sides. Remove from the skillet and set aside.
3. In the same skillet, add the chopped onion, minced garlic, and chopped bell pepper. Sauté until softened. Stir in the diced tomatoes, raisins, sliced olives, capers, white wine, Worcestershire sauce, soy sauce, tomato paste, ground cumin, paprika, salt, and pepper. Cook for a few minutes until the flavors meld together. Return the browned meats to the skillet and mix well with the vegetable mixture. Cook for an additional 10-15 minutes, stirring occasionally, until the filling is thick and flavorful. Remove from heat and let it cool.
4. Assemble the Hallacas: Lay out a piece of plantain leaf and spread a portion of the dough on top, shaping it into a rectangle. Place a generous spoonful of the filling in the center of the dough rectangle. Fold the sides of the plantain leaf over the filling to enclose it completely, then fold the top and bottom edges to seal the hallaca. Secure the hallaca with kitchen twine or toothpicks. Repeat the process with the remaining dough and filling.
5. Steam the hallacas: Steam the hallacas in a large pot or steamer for about 1-2 hours, or until the dough is cooked through and firm.
6. Serve the Hallacas Oriental hot, garnished with additional chopped fresh cilantro or parsley if desired.

Enjoy these delicious Hallacas Oriental as a traditional Venezuelan dish, incorporating flavors and ingredients from the eastern region of Venezuela! Adjust the filling ingredients and seasonings to suit your taste preferences.

Roscón de Reyes

Ingredients:

- 4 cups all-purpose flour
- 1/2 cup granulated sugar
- 1/2 teaspoon salt
- 1/2 cup warm milk
- 1/4 cup warm water
- 2 1/4 teaspoons active dry yeast (or 1 packet)
- 3 eggs
- Zest of 1 orange
- Zest of 1 lemon
- 1/4 cup unsalted butter, softened
- 1 teaspoon orange blossom water (optional)
- 1 teaspoon vanilla extract
- Candied fruits (such as orange peel, cherries, or figs), for decoration
- Sliced almonds, for decoration
- Powdered sugar, for dusting

Instructions:

1. In a small bowl, dissolve the yeast in warm water with a pinch of sugar. Let it sit for about 5-10 minutes, until foamy.
2. In a large mixing bowl, combine the flour, granulated sugar, and salt. Make a well in the center and add the warm milk, yeast mixture, eggs, orange zest, lemon zest, softened butter, orange blossom water (if using), and vanilla extract.
3. Mix the ingredients together until a dough forms. Knead the dough on a lightly floured surface for about 8-10 minutes, until it becomes smooth and elastic.
4. Place the dough in a greased bowl, cover with plastic wrap or a clean kitchen towel, and let it rise in a warm place for about 1-2 hours, or until it doubles in size.
5. Punch down the dough and transfer it to a lightly floured surface. Shape the dough into a ring, leaving a hole in the center.
6. Transfer the shaped dough to a parchment-lined baking sheet. Cover it loosely with plastic wrap or a clean kitchen towel and let it rise for another 30-60 minutes.
7. Preheat your oven to 375°F (190°C).
8. Once the dough has risen, decorate the top with candied fruits and sliced almonds.

9. Bake the Roscón de Reyes in the preheated oven for about 20-25 minutes, or until golden brown and cooked through.
10. Remove the Roscón from the oven and let it cool completely on a wire rack.
11. Once cooled, dust the Roscón with powdered sugar before serving.

Enjoy this delicious Roscón de Reyes as a festive treat to celebrate Epiphany! You can slice it and serve it with hot chocolate or coffee for a delightful dessert or breakfast on Three Kings' Day.

www.ingramcontent.com/pod-product-compliance
Lightning Source LLC
LaVergne TN
LVHW061945070526
838199LV00060B/3987